What Is a Liquid?

by Jennifer Boothroyd

first step nonfiction

Lerner Publications Company · Minneapolis

All things are made of **matter.**

Matter is anything that takes
up space.

3

There are three kinds of matter.

A **liquid** is a kind of matter.

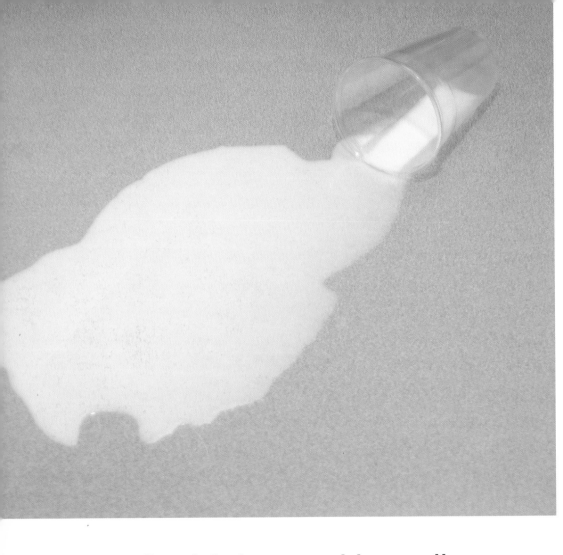

A liquid does not have its own shape.

A liquid takes the shape of
its container.

Water is a liquid. It flows.

Paint is a liquid. It drips.

Juice is a liquid. You can pour it.

Heating a liquid can change it.

Heating can change a liquid
into a **gas.**

Water becomes **steam.**

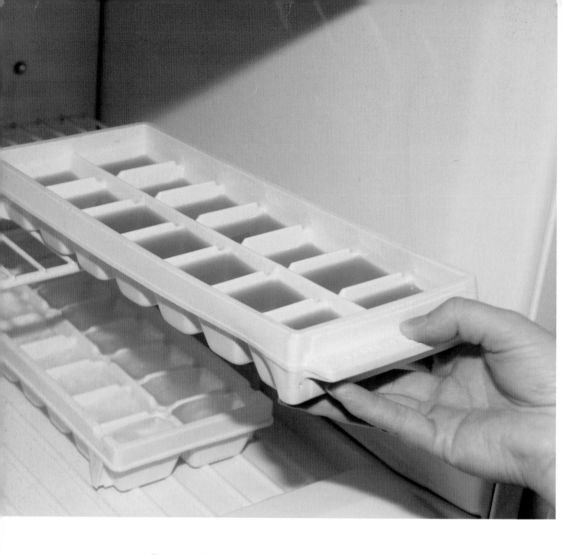

Cooling a liquid can
change it.

Cooling can change a liquid
into a **solid.**

15

Water freezes into ice.

Look around. What liquids do you see?

Which one has the most liquid?

Look at the picture. Which container has the most liquid in it? Did you pick the vase? This was a trick question. All three containers have the same amount of liquid. Liquids take the shape of their containers. The shape and size of a container may make it look like it has more or less liquid than other containers do. Try this experiment: pour the same amount of liquid into different-sized containers. Does it look like they have different amounts of liquid in them?

Fun Facts

When some liquids are mixed together, they make a new liquid. Chocolate milk is one example.

Some liquids do not make a new liquid when they are mixed together. Oil and water will stay separate in a jar.

Liquids can be thick or thin. Thick liquids like honey and syrup flow slowly. Thin liquids like water and juice flow quickly.

Evaporation happens when a liquid dries up. The liquid changes to a gas and becomes part of the air.

On some mornings, everything outside is covered with drops of water. These drops are called dew. Dew forms when the water in the air cools and changes from a gas into a liquid.

On very cold days, dew freezes. It becomes a solid called frost.

Glossary

 gas – something that is not a liquid and takes the shape of its container

 liquid – something that flows

 matter – anything that takes up space

 solid – something that has a definite shape

 steam – water that has become a gas

Index

The photographs in this book are used with the permission of: © Photodisc/Photodisc Green/Getty Images, front cover; PhotoDisc Royalty Free by Getty Images, pp. 2, 3, 4 (right), 8, 13, 22 (middle, bottom); © Todd Strand/Independent Picture Service, pp. 4 (top), 6, 9, 14; © Ryan McVay/Photodisc Green/Getty Images, pp. 4 (bottom), 5, 22 (second from top); Comstock Images, p. 7; © Sam Lund/Independent Picture Service, p. 10; © Nana Twumasi/Independent Picture Service, pp. 11, 12, 22 (top); © Marta Johnson/Independent Picture Service, pp. 15, 22 (second from bottom); © Michael T. Sedam/CORBIS, p. 16; © Buccina Studios/Photodisc Blue/Getty Images, p. 17; © Erica Johnson/Independent Picture Service, p. 18.

Lerner Publications Company
a division of Lerner Publishing Group
241 First Avenue North
Minneapolis, MN 55401 U.S.A.

Website address: www.lernerbooks.com

Library of Congress Cataloging-in-Publication Data

Boothroyd, Jennifer, 1972–
    What is a liquid? / by Jennifer Boothroyd.
      p.   cm. — (First step nonfiction)
    Includes index.
    ISBN-13: 978–0–8225–6838–4 (lib. bdg. : alk. paper)
    ISBN-10: 0–8225–6838–1 (lib. bdg. : alk. paper)
    1. Liquids—Juvenile literature.   2. Fluid mechanics—Juvenile literature.   I. Title.
  II. Series.
  QC145.24.B66 2007
  530.4'2—dc22   2006006304

Manufactured in the United States of America
1 2 3 4 5 6 – DP – 12 11 10 09 08 07